To find out more about Jason Pruett,
visit his website at www.jasonpruett.com

© 2024 Jason Pruett
All rights reserved.

No part of this book may be reproduced in any form whatsoever, whether by graphic, visual, electronic, film, microfilm, tape recording, or any other means, without prior written permission of the author, except in the case of brief passages embodied in critical reviews and articles.

This book is not an official publication of The Church of Jesus Christ of Latter-day Saints.

ISBN: 978-1-4621-4818-9

Published by CFI, an imprint of Cedar Fort, Inc.
2373 W. 700 S., Suite 100, Springville, UT 84663
Distributed by Cedar Fort, Inc., www.cedarfort.com

Library of Congress Control Number: 2014950527

Cover design by Shawnda T. Craig
Cover design © 2024 Cedar Fort, Inc.
Edited by Kevin Haws

Printed in China

10 9 8 7 6 5 4 3 2 1

Printed on acid-free paper

CFI
An Imprint of Cedar Fort, Inc.
Springville, Utah

The Introduction

The beginning of the Book of Mormon has an introduction, testimonies of people who saw the golden plates, Joseph Smith's story of how he received the golden plates (which he then translated into English through the power of God), and a brief explanation of the plates.

Seek & Find

- ☐ Book in an arch (keystone)—Introduction
- ☐ The Three Witnesses—Testimony of Three Witnesses
- ☐ The Eight Witnesses—Testimony of Eight Witnesses
- ☐ Joseph using a lever to move a rock—Testimony of the Prophet Joseph Smith
- ☐ People trying to get the plates from Joseph in various ways—Testimony of the Prophet Joseph Smith

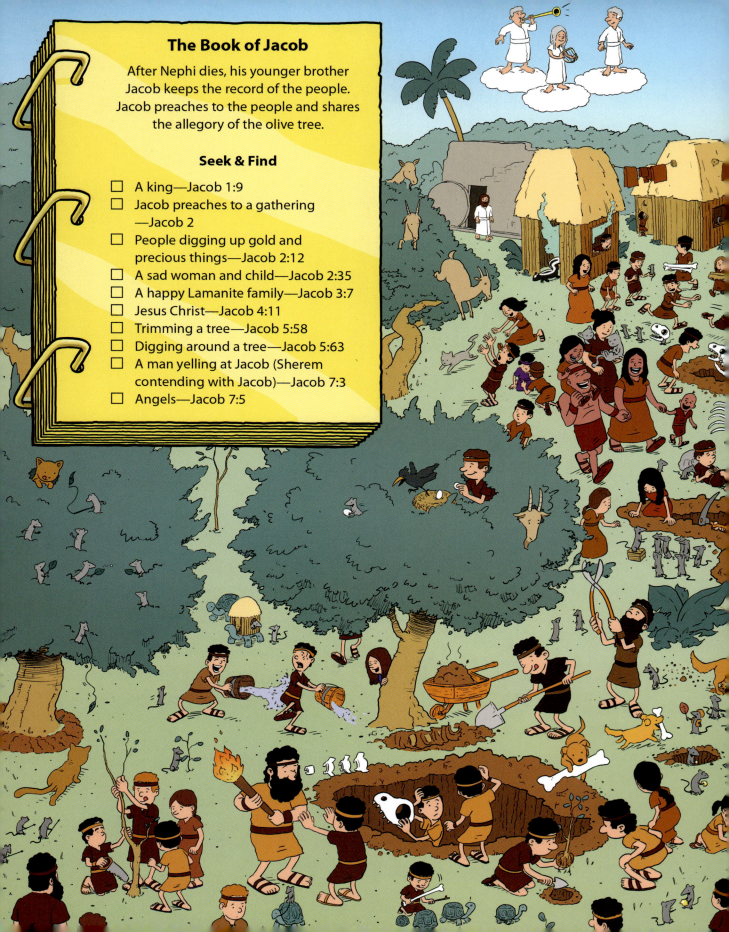

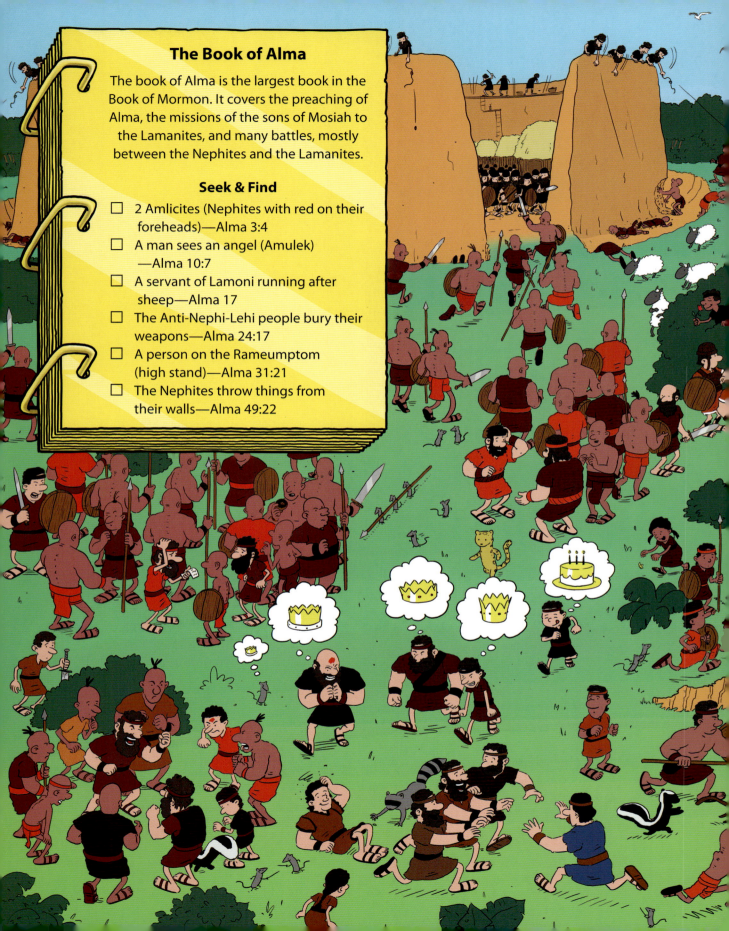

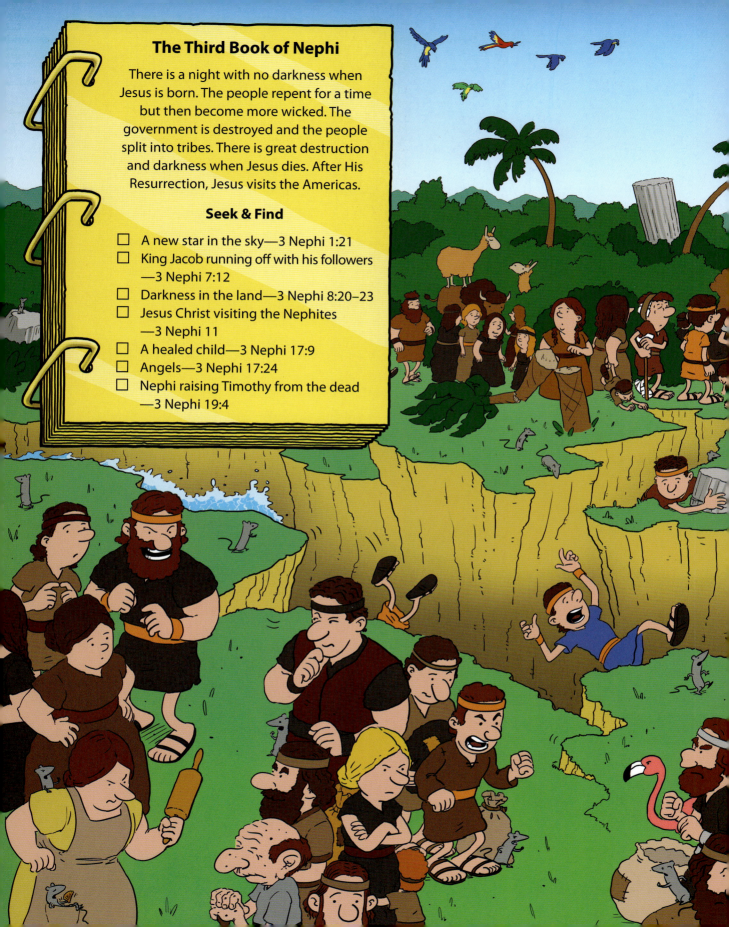

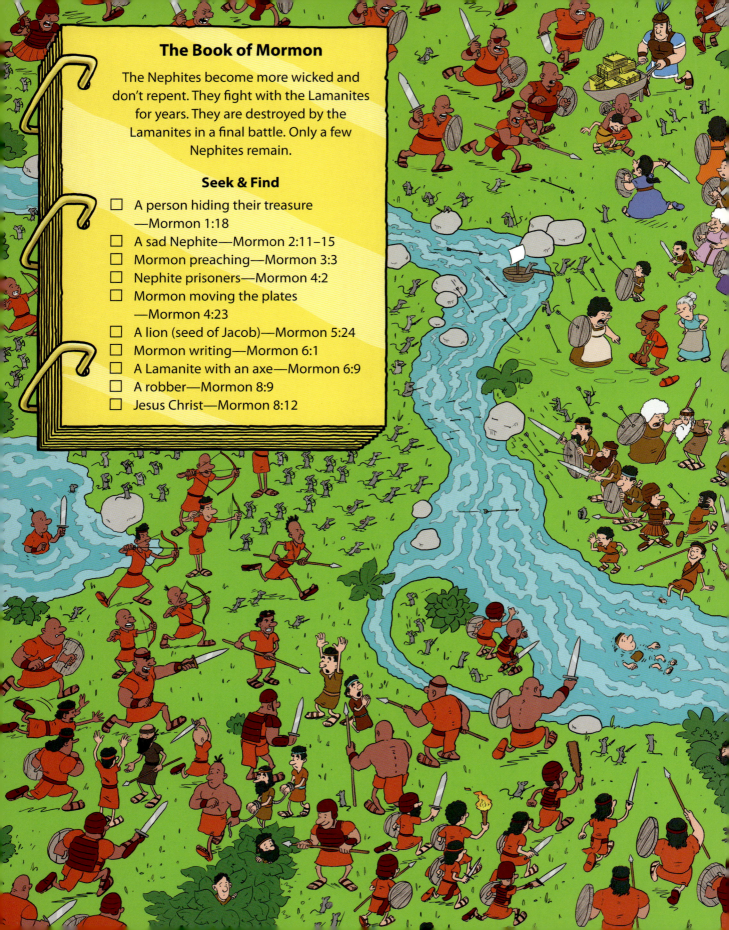

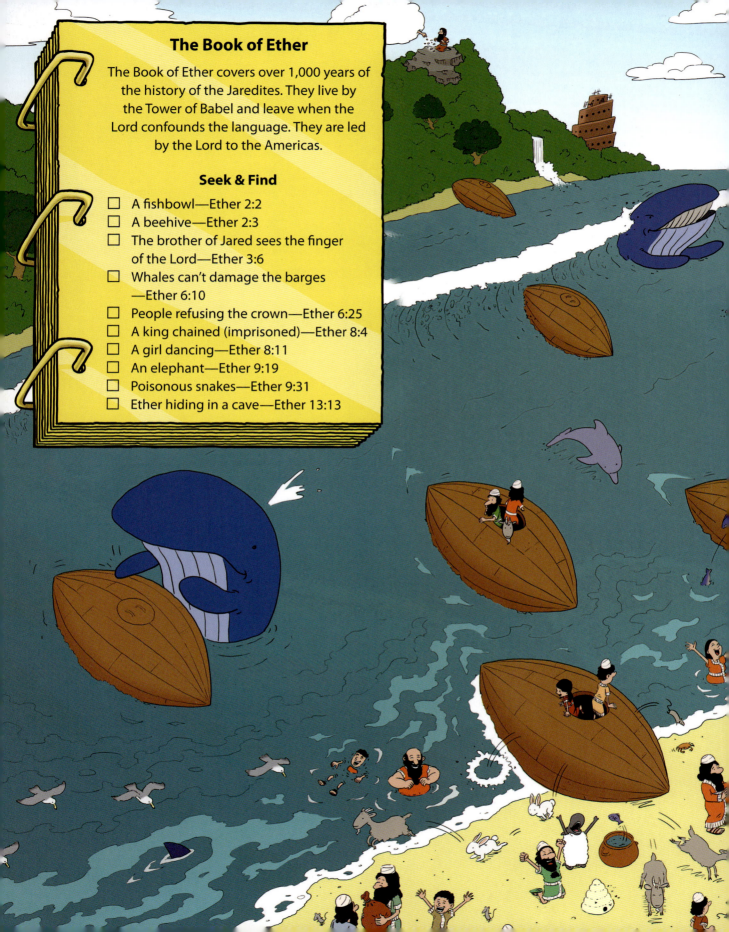

The Book of Ether

The Book of Ether covers over 1,000 years of the history of the Jaredites. They live by the Tower of Babel and leave when the Lord confounds the language. They are led by the Lord to the Americas.

Seek & Find

- ☐ A fishbowl—Ether 2:2
- ☐ A beehive—Ether 2:3
- ☐ The brother of Jared sees the finger of the Lord—Ether 3:6
- ☐ Whales can't damage the barges—Ether 6:10
- ☐ People refusing the crown—Ether 6:25
- ☐ A king chained (imprisoned)—Ether 8:4
- ☐ A girl dancing—Ether 8:11
- ☐ An elephant—Ether 9:19
- ☐ Poisonous snakes—Ether 9:31
- ☐ Ether hiding in a cave—Ether 13:13

More items to seek & find . . .

Introduction
- [ ] A pig walking a pig
- [ ] A rat stealing an egg
- [ ] A horse lifting its hat
- [ ] A fake cow
- [ ] Fish out of water
- [ ] A rat riding a chicken

First Nephi
- [ ] A dog catcher
- [ ] A donkey stealing fruit
- [ ] Animals celebrating
- [ ] A person hiding in a basket
- [ ] Rats climbing ladders
- [ ] A camel climbing a wall
- [ ] Someone getting tickled
- [ ] Birds playing chess

Second Nephi
- [ ] Birds fighting with swords
- [ ] A rat going for a ride
- [ ] A man tripping over a tree stump
- [ ] A beehive
- [ ] A sheep waving
- [ ] A sheep laughing
- [ ] An armadillo with a guitar
- [ ] Someone stepping on a rat's tail

Jacob
- [ ] A beehive
- [ ] A rat running off with a dog's bone
- [ ] A dog taking a break
- [ ] Dinosaur bones
- [ ] Gold plates
- [ ] A rat zip line
- [ ] Goats in trees

Enos, Jarom, and Omni
- [ ] A wolf in sheep's clothing
- [ ] 3 beehives
- [ ] A rat riding a rabbit
- [ ] Someone dropping a coconut
- [ ] People playing tug-of-war
- [ ] A rat with a carrot
- [ ] Some painters
- [ ] A sheep with its tongue out

Words of Mormon
- [ ] A beehive
- [ ] The alphabet
- [ ] 10 cats
- [ ] A piece of cake
- [ ] Pancakes
- [ ] A cat who won't move
- [ ] Turtle race
- [ ] A rat drawing on a sheep's face
- [ ] A cat throwing something
- [ ] A rat carrying small plates

Mosiah
- [ ] A beehive
- [ ] 6 crowns
- [ ] Rat musicians
- [ ] Someone playing hopscotch
- [ ] A guard leaning on someone
- [ ] A scarecrow
- [ ] A tired traveler

Alma
- [ ] 2 beehives
- [ ] 4 crowns
- [ ] Someone getting kissed on the cheek
- [ ] A skunk chasing a cat
- [ ] Rats with a spear

Helaman
- [ ] Three carrots
- [ ] A beehive
- [ ] Fish out of water
- [ ] A rat walking on a tightrope
- [ ] Rats doing pull-ups
- [ ] Someone dropping an egg
- [ ] A man missing a tooth

Third Nephi
- [ ] A person eating
- [ ] Bigfoot
- [ ] A beehive
- [ ] Rats with dominoes
- [ ] A rat with a fan
- [ ] A flamingo
- [ ] A bear in line
- [ ] A mouse jumping for cheese
- [ ] A llama standing on a bison

Fourth Nephi
- [ ] 2 beehives
- [ ] Rats taking cookies
- [ ] Toasting marshmallows
- [ ] A rat rolling a barrel
- [ ] 2 pies
- [ ] A raccoon stealing a hat
- [ ] A rat and a cat sharing a cookie
- [ ] A boy sticking out his tongue
- [ ] An armadillo
- [ ] A bison

Mormon
- [ ] A woman telling a Lamanite to take off his dirty sandals
- [ ] A beehive
- [ ] 2 vultures
- [ ] A Nephite juggling
- [ ] 2 rats jousting
- [ ] A cat with a shield
- [ ] 2 frogs
- [ ] A torch
- [ ] A Lamanite running on heads
- [ ] A man biting someone
- [ ] A man with an eyepatch

Ether
- [ ] A rat in a boat
- [ ] 3 crowns
- [ ] A shark fin
- [ ] Hair being pulled
- [ ] People running into each other
- [ ] Whales playing football
- [ ] Someone jumping into hay
- [ ] Someone making a sand angel

Moroni
- [ ] A snake squeezing a Lamanite
- [ ] Someone with a bird headdress
- [ ] Someone being held upside down by his ankles
- [ ] A Lamanite in a hammock
- [ ] Snakes in a backpack
- [ ] An upset jaguar
- [ ] Bigfoot
- [ ] A beehive
- [ ] A pig
- [ ] A Nephite running
- [ ] A rat with a telescope
- [ ] Someone with a lot of spears
- [ ] A Lamanite scared by a snake
- [ ] A rat on someone's head